A Teddy Horsley I

The W

Betsy Bear senses God's Care

Based on Psalm 23

by Leslie J Francis and Nicola M Slee
Pictures by Laura Cooper

Bible Society

The Bear facts:
The Teddy Horsley Bible Series is designed to build bridges between the young child's day to day experiences of the world and major biblical themes and stories.

Both authors work in church-linked colleges concerned with Teacher Education. Nicola Slee lectures in Religious Studies at Whitelands College in London. Leslie Francis is Research Fellow at Trinity College in Carmarthen.

The Teddy Horsley Series is a result of both authors' extensive research into the religious development of young children and their wide experience of educational work in schools and churches.

BIBLE SOCIETY
Stonehill Green, Westlea, SWINDON SN5 7DG, England
Series editor: David Martin
Text © Leslie J Francis and Nicola M Slee 1989
Illustrations © Bible Society 1989

Unless otherwise stated, quotations from the Bible are from the Good News Bible, published by the Bible Societies/Collins, © American Bible Society, New York, 1966, 1971, 1976.

First published 1989   ISBN 0 564 05345 7   Printed in Hong Kong

Betsy Bear likes to go walking with Mr and Mrs Henry, Lucy, Walter, and Teddy Horsley.

Sometimes they walk to the railway,
where trains clatter past.

The guard tells Betsy where to stand
so she will be safe.

Sometimes they walk in the country,
where fields unfold for miles.

The farmer points out the signpost to Betsy
so she will not lose her way.

Sometimes they walk by the canal,
where boats sway in the water.

The lock-keeper shows Betsy the path
so she will not fall in.

Sometimes they walk in the park,
where dogs chase and play.

The park-keeper stays close to Betsy's side
so she will not get hurt.

Sometimes they walk in the town,
where crowds and cars rush by.

The policewoman leads Betsy across the road so the traffic will not harm her.

Sometimes they walk to the school,
where children run in the playground.

The teacher keeps an eye on Betsy
so she will not get pushed over.

Everywhere she walks in the wide, wide world, Betsy Bear knows her friends are there to watch over her.

Betsy Bear likes to go walking with Mr and
Mrs Henry, Lucy, Walter, and Teddy Horsley.

She hears the noisy trains zip past,
but she is not afraid.

She sees the country lanes disappear into the distance, but she knows she will not get lost.

She peers down into the deep water of the canal,
but she is not frightened.

She watches the playful dogs chase in the park,
but she knows she will not be harmed.

She feels the crowds push past her in the street,
but she does not worry.

She sees the children run and shout in school,
but she knows she is safe.

Everywhere she walks in the wide, wide world,
Betsy Bear knows God is there to watch over her.

In *The Walk*, Betsy Bear's experience of being cared for and protected from danger brings alive the sense of God's providing care in Psalm 23:

The LORD is my shepherd;
I have everything I need.
He lets me rest in fields of green grass
and leads me to quiet pools of fresh water.
He gives me new strength.
He guides me in the right paths,
as he has promised.
Even if I go through the deepest darkness,
I will not be afraid, LORD,
for you are with me.
Your shepherd's rod and staff protect me.

Psalm 23. 1-4

The following questions suggest further ways of developing the links between the young child's experience, the story and the Bible passage.

Talk about going for walks:
Where do you like to go walking?
Who do you like to go walking with?
Who do you meet when you go walking?
Have you ever got lost or hurt yourself when you were out for a walk? What happened? Who looked after you?

Talk about the story:
Where did Betsy Bear go walking?
What did she see? What did she do? Who did she meet?
How did she know she would be safe?

Think some more about the story:
Where else might Betsy Bear go walking?
What would she see? What would she do? Who would she meet?
How would she keep safe?

Titles in the series

Good Morning

The Grumpy Day

The Present

The Walk

Lights

The Explorer

Night-Time

Do and Tell

Music Makers

The Windy Day

The Sunny Morning

Neighbours

Other publications to help young children explore the Bible:

Bible Storyboards — Wooden play-tray jigsaws, which present a Bible story in six scenes with ''lift-out'' characters, ''match-up'' pictures, and story-telling script. Designed to encourage learning through play.

Open House Books — Six house-shaped board books focussing on the homes of well known Bible characters. Simple storylines relate Bible stories associated with each place.

Bible Storygraphics — A video giving ten-minute presentations of three well known Bible stories using narration, music, and computer-generated graphics.